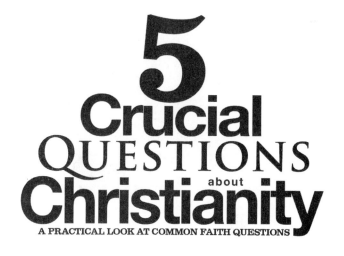

5 Crucial QUESTIONS about Christianity

A PRACTICAL LOOK AT COMMON FAITH QUESTIONS

Tom Short

Tom Short
CAMPUS MINISTRIES

ww.5CrucialQuestions.com

5 Crucial Questions about Christianity, by Tom Short
Copyright © 2001
www.5CrucialQuestions.com

Tom Short Campus Ministries
PO Box 224
Worthington, OH 43085
www.TomthePreacher.com

Printed in the United States of America
Published by Tom Short Campus Ministries
Columbus, Ohio

ISBN# 9-780971-419803
Fifth Printing, 2013

Edited by Jan Warren
Cover design and layout by Timothy Short

Contents

Introduction

A large crowd had gathered to hear me speak at Texas A&M University. One student in particular, an atheist, couldn't accept anything I had to say about Christianity. I've forgotten her name, but I'll never forget her story. Since I'm always curious how people arrive at their beliefs, I asked her how she had become an atheist.

"I was raised to believe in God," she began, "but when I got to middle school, I began to have questions about what I was being taught in church. When I asked my priest about them, he couldn't answer me. Instead, he just told me to have faith, that it was wrong and sinful of me to doubt and ask questions. I suppressed my questions for many years, but when I came to college, I discovered other people had the same questions. After talking with them, I found that they were all either atheists or agnostics. And so I became one, too."

No one could fault her for concluding that Christianity didn't have the answers to her tough questions. However, the truth is that Christianity *does* have answers to her tough questions – it's just that many well-meaning people (including many theologians and church leaders) have never taken the time to find the answers!

Unfortunately, I'm afraid this young woman's experience might be all too common. There is a general perception that while Christians are apparently nice people who seem to have found something that gives them inner peace, security and happiness, their beliefs simply can't stand up to intellectual scrutiny.

Nothing could be further from the truth! If you stick with me through this short book, I will address crucial questions that people ask about Christianity and provide you with *reasons* to believe in Christ – reasons that you may have never thought about.

Incompatible?

"Wait a minute," you may say. "What's all this talk about reason? I thought Christianity was based on faith. Aren't reason and faith incompatible?"

Actually, they're not. It's true that a person needs faith to be a Christian. The Bible says that "without faith it is impossible to please Him, for everyone who comes to God must believe that He is, and that He is a rewarder of those who seek Him" (Hebrews 11:6). Faith is to believe – or trust – in someone or something you have never seen.

But that doesn't mean that faith is contrary to reason, logic and evidence.

In fact, true faith is often very reasonable and based on sound evidence. Christianity is a thinking person's religion. It does not call us to be naïve or gullible, but instead it appeals to our minds as well as our hearts. After all, God gave each of us a brain and He intends for us to use it!

Perhaps an illustration will help show the correlation between faith (trust) and evidence. Picture yourself living on the tenth floor of an apartment building when the fire alarm sounds. You hurry to the stairwell only to find it full of smoke. You rush back to your room, put a wet towel under the crack in the door and try to figure out how to escape.

As your room begins to fill with smoke, you open the window, stand on the ledge and remember what your Sunday School teacher taught you as a little kid: "If you believe strongly enough, you can do anything." So, as you stand on the window ledge and look down ten stories, you try to convince yourself that if you flap your arms hard enough and believe that you can fly, then you can.

"I believe I can fly, I believe I can fly," you tell yourself. But we all know that no matter how hard you flap your arms and no matter how strongly you believe, if you jump from that ledge you are jumping to your death. All the *faith* in the world won't enable you to fly. I contend that this isn't the kind of faith that God wants you to have. This kind of "faith" really is stupid – and might be hazardous to your health as well!

Now let's consider a slightly different scenario. Your apartment building is on fire and you discover there is no way to safety except through the window. Only this time you go to the ledge and – lo and behold! – down on the ground below you the fire department has set up a huge net. A burly fireman yells up to you through his bullhorn, "Jump and we'll catch you!"

You are now faced with a decision that will test your faith – not your faith in God, but your faith in the firefighters. You have to decide whether or not you trust these people. Will they be able to catch you? Will their equipment work? You're putting your life in their hands, and you wouldn't do that without faith (trust) in them. You've never jumped from a ten-story building before, but if you decide that these firefighters are trustworthy, you'll take a "leap of faith" – literally!

Everyday faith

By viewing faith in this context, you'll see that much of what we do every day depends on faith, or trust, in others. Every time you drink a can of pop, you exercise faith in the bottling company. Every time you drive your car down the road, you exercise faith in the company that made your car and in the other drivers you share the road with – generally drivers you've never even met before.

You exercise faith in your professor and the textbooks you use in class. You exercise faith in your bank when you deposit your hard-earned money. You have faith (trust) in your relationships with others, and you feel offended if others don't have faith in you.

Almost every human interaction involves faith. Is it really that unusual that God would expect us to have faith (trust) in Him as well?

Yes, you must have faith, but there is nothing more reasonable than to have faith in God. That is the thesis of this little book. Since faith is essential, I would like to ask you to talk to God in faith for just a moment. Just take a minute right now and ask God to help you get the answers you need in your life as you read this book. You might want to say something like this:

> *Dear God, I want to know the truth about you. I ask you to reveal your truth and yourself to me. As I read, help me to understand what you have to say to me. Help me to have faith and trust in you and come to know your love and forgiveness in a personal way. Thank you for hearing my prayer. Amen.*

Now let's start looking at those crucial questions!

Note on the 2013 edition:
Look for these icons to provide in-depth video content.
Visit TomthePreacher.com

QUESTION 1

Is there really evidence that God exists?

The professor greeted his class with an unusual request. "If you're a Christian, I want you to stand up," he announced.

A handful of students rose to their feet, sheepishly looking around at one another and wondering why they had been singled out.

"How many of you have ever *seen* God?" the professor asked. He was met with absolute silence.

"Have any of you ever *heard* God speak to you?" he continued. More silence.

Becoming somewhat bolder, he threw out a final question, "Have any of you ever *smelled* God, *tasted* God or *touched* God?" Again, the Christian students stood in silence.

"I didn't think so," he announced rather smugly. "Now I want you to remember something. This is a science class. We don't believe in anything here unless we have seen, heard, smelled, tasted or touched it. So as far as I'm concerned, God doesn't even exist. Now sit down, and don't let me hear about your God for the rest of the semester."

Intimidated, the students quietly took their seats. That is, all but one. Noticing the lone student still on his feet, the professor frowned slightly. "What do you want?" he asked.

"Before I sit down, I was wondering if I could ask you a question," the student replied. "Sir, have you ever seen, heard, smelled, tasted or touched your own brain?"

"Of course not," the professor responded. "Why do you ask?"

"Because based on your previous ground rules, I must conclude that you don't have one!" the student replied, wisely taking his seat. (Don't ask me what grade he received that semester!)

A no-brainer

The truth is that we *all* believe in many things that we haven't personally seen, heard, smelled, tasted or touched. At this very moment, you are surrounded by radio waves that you would never know existed if you relied solely on your five natural senses. Have you ever seen an atom? How about gravity? For that matter, have you ever seen the wind?

Every day people are convicted of crimes based on over-whelming evidence that they are guilty – crimes that no one *saw* them commit! We believe in historical events because other people have reported what happened, not because we saw them for ourselves. Indeed, most of what we believe about history, geography, science – even current events – we believe based on someone else's testimony rather than our own personal observation.

Likewise, just as there is evidence for radio waves, gravity, wind – and, yes, even that professor's brain – one must ask if there is evidence for the existence of God. I believe there is.

Where did it all come from?

Have you ever met a watchmaker? Most of us haven't. And yet, do you know that watchmakers exist? Of course you do! How do you know? You look at your wrist, see your watch and you conclude that this marvelous little instrument couldn't have come into being on its own. It had to have been made by someone. That someone is called a watchmaker.

You can repeat this same exercise by looking at a building and knowing that there are architects, engineers and carpenters. Look at a car and you can conclude that there are automakers. Look at a book and you'll conclude that there are authors. It matters not whether you have ever met such people; their product is proof of their existence.

And just as a watch is evidence of a watchmaker, a building is evidence of an architect, and a book is evidence of an author, in the same way, the creation is evidence of a creator.

This is one of the most basic laws of science – the law of cause and effect. But looking at the creation tells us more than merely that a creator exists. It also tells us something about that creator.

Consider, for instance, that the first cause of limitless space must be infinite. The first cause of unlimited energy must be omnipotent (all powerful). The first cause of infinite complexity must by omniscient (all knowing). And the first cause of endless time must be eternal.

Suddenly, we begin to recognize what this creator must be like – infinite, all powerful, all knowing and eternal.

But the creation demonstrates even more than this, showing further that the first cause of life must be living (not just an energy force or "higher power"). The first cause of love must be loving (not an impersonal being). And the first cause of justice must be just (the source of our sense of right and wrong).

Suddenly, we discover that the creation around us tells us some very specific things about the Creator and refines our concept of God considerably. We not only see that God exists, but that He is a living, personal, and moral being.

Who made the Maker?

Unfortunately, the skeptic is not persuaded. He usually tries to skirt the issue by asking, "If everything needs a maker, then who made God?"

The answer is simple: "No one made God!" God is eternal and self-existing. When we say that every effect has a cause, we are referring to the physical universe. But God is spirit – His realm is outside of the physical. Just as God is not subject to the law of gravity or the space-time continuum, He is also not subject to the physical law of cause and effect.

Others might respond by saying that everything got here by means of evolution and chance. While I don't want to get into the finer details of the evolution/creation debate at this time, suffice it to say that even most people who do believe in evolution still believe that God had to guide the process.

▶ Tom Short:
Who Created God?
You Tube

After all, consider the chances of life forming on its own. Scientists have come up with some fascinating illustrations.

Cosmic proportions

Francis Crick, who co-discovered DNA, calculated the possibility of 200 amino acids forming on their own at 10 followed by 260 zeros! That number is more than the estimated number of atoms in our entire solar system!

The great astrophysicist Sir Fredrick Hoyle calculates the odds of biological life evolving on its own as comparable to 1,000,000,000,000,000,000,000,000,000,000,000,000, 000,000,000,000,000 *blind* people all solving a Rubik's Cube at the exact same moment! Hoyle goes on to claim that life forming on its own would be less likely than a tornado going through a junk yard and forming a 747 airplane!

Roger Penrose, who helped develop Black Hole theories, estimated the odds of a "big bang" forming an orderly universe to be one in 100,000,000,000 to the 123rd power. This is similar to the odds of hitting a one-inch target on the other side of the universe or to the odds of a pole-vaulter's pole standing on its tip for centuries following a vault!

Indeed, those who are pure naturalists – who believe that evolution explains our origins without any involvement by God – have a couple of other tough questions to answer.

For example, how did inorganic material become alive? Do we have any actual evidence that this has ever happened?

As we observe nature, we understand that matter tends to become disorganized over time (entropy). If the world was created without intervention, how did matter become so well organized all by itself? Does chaos + time = order?

There are plenty of other questions as well, but these two focus on the reality that life in our universe is extremely complex and well formed – far too complex to have happened without an intelligent being behind it all. That intelligent being is known as "God."

Cultural evidence

Have you noticed that every culture that has ever been discovered believed in some kind of superior spiritual being? While different peoples might disagree on exactly who that being is or what that being is like, there has never been a single culture in the history of the world that didn't acknowledge some sort of supreme being. It is certainly reasonable to ask, would all of humankind universally believe in something that simply wasn't there?

Perhaps an example of how people simply don't believe the unbelievable would be in order. When I was growing up, we Americans feared the very real possibility of nuclear war.

> ● Tom Short:
> **What about those of other religions?**
> You Tube

We even had drills at school on what to do in case of a nuclear attack. We feared that attack, if it came, would come from the Soviets or perhaps from Cuba. To my knowledge, no one ever had a practice drill on what to do if Haiti launched a nuclear strike on the United States. Why? Because Haiti didn't have nukes! You can't launch what you don't have.

The mass of people will contemplate the *possible*, not the *impossible*. Likewise, the fact that the vast majority of people throughout history have contemplated God and the afterlife is, to me, evidence that God and the afterlife are real.

The existence of miracles is another evidence of God's existence. I'm not talking about the "miracle of a sunrise" or "the miracle of birth." I'm talking about a real miracle where something happened that violated natural laws and that had no scientific explanation – where God Himself intervened in human history.

Perhaps you have never witnessed a miracle, but there are multitudes who would swear that they have. Of course, miracles – by their very definition – would be rare and contrary to natural law. But God loves people and desires to be involved in their lives for their good. As you open up your life to Him and open your eyes to look carefully, you just might see miracles in your life as well. (I have more to say on this subject in chapter 3.)

Speaking of atheists...

As we have seen, when debating the existence of God, the evidence is on the side of those who believe, not on the side of those who deny the reality of God. In fact, I'll go so far as to claim that to be an atheist is to hold an irrational and intellectually indefensible position. Let me explain.

There are three positions a person can take concerning the existence of God:

> *Theism*, which claims that God exists;

Agnosticism, which claims that you cannot know whether or not God exists; and

Atheism, which claims that God does not exist.

Let me demonstrate how position 3 (atheism) is not really rational. Suppose I tell a group of people that I have hidden a rare silver dollar somewhere in the city and send them out to look for it.

When everyone returns several hours later, some people happily claim to have found the silver dollar. These folks represent theists (position 1).

Other people claim to be confused, stating that they looked but could not find the silver dollar. They do, however, acknowledge that the city is quite large and that the silver dollar might be hidden someplace where they haven't looked. Therefore, they couldn't say whether the silver dollar is – or is not – hidden in the city. This group represents agnostics (position 2).

A third group claims that they have looked for the silver dollar – but since they cannot find it, it simply doesn't exist. These people represent atheists (position 3).

Even though other people claim to have found the silver dollar, the "atheists" in effect write them off as either being deceived or confused. When other people plead with them to keep looking, the "atheists" tell them that the effort is a waste of time. When asked if they have searched every nook and cranny in the city, the "atheists" say they don't need to – they have looked enough to know that the silver dollar simply doesn't exist!

Fuzzy logic

You can see how, in this story, the conclusions of the first two groups are intellectually defensible, but the conclusion of group three is not. I guess this is why the great atheist Isaac Asimov once admitted, "For years I tried to be an atheist for intellectual reasons. Finally, I realized that is impossible. I, therefore, became an atheist purely for emotional reasons."

And what were those "emotional reasons" for denying what he couldn't deny intellectually? Asimov didn't say. Perhaps he felt that God had mistreated him, let him down or didn't love him. Perhaps he knew that believing in God would mean admitting that he had certain moral responsibilities that he didn't want to face. Who knows? The important thing is to make sure that *you* don't let an "emotional reason" keep you from acknowledging that God exists.

And, if God does exist, can you think of anything more important than discovering who He is and what a great life He has for you? I can't! So let's get right on to chapter 2, where we'll discover how to find the answer to this all-important question.

QUESTION 2

Isn't the Bible just another book?

Actually, nothing could be further from the truth. By any standard of measurement chosen, the Bible would distinguish itself as the most unique book of all time. Consider the following:

The Bible was the first book ever printed on a printing press. In 1454, Johannes Gutenberg turned a winepress into a printing press and printed the Bible. Thus, one of the world's most significant inventions was developed to promote the reading and availability of the Bible.

Since that day in 1454, it has remained the most published book of all time. In 1930, the one billionth Bible was printed, a number now duplicated every five years. Contrast this with the amazing success of the Harry Potter books, which in the summer of 2,000 broke all publishing records with first-week sales of 3.8 million copies.

And yet, there are over 3.8 million copies of the Bible printed and distributed *each week* – week after week, month after month, year after year, decade after decade. There's never been another book like it!

The Bible has been translated into over 2,400 languages and dialects – and the number grows each month. The second most translated book of all time is *The Diary of Ann Frank*, which can be read in 67 different languages. Once again, the Bible stands head and shoulders above every other book ever written.

> ▶ Tom Short:
> **How can you believe a book that has been translated so many times?**
>
>

A source of inspiration

The Bible has inspired many of the world's greatest scientific achievements. Despite the alleged conflict between science and religion, the Bible itself has served as the inspiration to great scientists such as Blaise Pascal, Charles Babbage, Galileo, Michael Faraday, Robert Boyle, Lord Kelvin, Johannes Kepler, Joseph Lister, Samuel Morse, Matthew Maury, Isaac Newton, Carl Von Linnaeus – the list is almost endless.

The Bible has inspired many great social movements. Efforts to establish higher education, increase literacy, abolish slavery, gain civil rights and care for the poor and oppressed all find their foundation in the Bible.

The Bible has inspired great political advancements. Whether it was fighting the Inquisition, casting off tyranny in the founding of our nation or overthrowing communism in Eastern Europe, the Bible has often played a major role in the expansion of freedom.

The Bible has been the foundation of our moral, ethical and legal code. The Ten Commandments, the Golden Rule, the Sermon on the Mount, the Love Chapter (1 Corinthians 13 – "Love is patient, love is kind...") all give us a simple, yet profound basis for moral behavior that has never been equaled.

The Bible is the most persecuted book of all time. In fact, not only have governments persecuted people for believing the Bible, but there were even times when a church would have you burned at the stake if you were found with a Bible in your possession!

More time, money and effort has gone into discrediting the Bible than any other book ever written and yet today, more people believe it than at any other time in history.

More people have found spiritual comfort, guidance and peace in the Bible than in any other book. It has been a source of strength, life and restoration to multitudes. It has, undoubtedly, had a greater effect on more people than any other book ever written.

Of course, the fame and influence of the Bible doesn't make it true. But it does give it a credibility that other books simply can't match. Just about any way you cut it, you have to conclude that the Bible is more than "just another book." In fact, it is the most amazing and influential book ever written.

Who wrote the Bible?

The Bible actually is a collection of 66 books (39 in the Old Testament, 27 in the New Testament). It was written by about 40 different writers who lived and wrote over a span of 1,500 years. They came from all walks of life – one was a king, another was a shepherd, yet another was a physician. Others were fishermen, historians, prophets and theologians. There was even an IRS agent (Matthew, the tax collector)!

Parts of the Bible were written while the authors were in the worst of circumstances (in prison, in great suffering, facing death) and other parts were written at the heights of happiness (after victory in battle, at a wedding feast, at the birth of a child).

They wrote in three separate languages; the Old Testament was written primarily in Hebrew with a short portion in Aramaic while the New Testament was written in Greek.

Most of the writers never met another writer of the Bible. And yet, the Bible reads as a single unfolding story about God's relationship with people. You would almost think that there was only one author. Indeed, if you thought so, you would be right, for behind these 40 human authors stands the real author of the Bible – God.

> ▶ Tom Short:
> **How can fallible men write an infallible book?**
>
> You Tube

At least, this is what the writers of the Bible claim. Over 2,000 times they prefaced their statements with comments like, "Thus says the Lord." They referred to themselves as prophets, or spokesmen, for God. They operated as if they had the awesome responsibility of communicating God's message to the world.

But did they? Were they well-meaning but deluded? Perhaps they were mere imposters – liars rather than prophets? Or were they, as they claimed, people God chose to use to reach out to humanity – even to you and me?

Personally, I've met only a very few people who believe these writers were intentional liars. Their writings have inspired the highest standards of integrity and honesty in others – extremely unlikely for a pack of liars! In addition, they seemed to have understood the gravity of what they were claiming for themselves. They lived in a culture where there was no greater obligation than to honor God. To falsely claim to be a prophet was a crime punishable by death. They accepted their calling with deep humility and sober responsibility.

Could they have been well-meaning, but deluded? Obviously anyone can think he is right and still be wrong. However, the accounts given to us by the Bible writers were couched in history. The writers claimed to be eyewitnesses of numerous events – even miraculous events – and asked us to accept the spiritual truths in light of the credibility they established in reporting the historical truths. In reporting these historical truths, they could not have been well-meaning but wrong. Either what they said happened or it didn't.

For instance, the followers of Jesus claimed, among other things, that He turned water into wine, healed a lame man and died on the cross. These events either happened or they didn't. If they didn't, then these writers were not well-meaning – they were lying.

This leaves only one option: if the writers were not intentional deceivers, they must have been truthful witnesses of God's miraculous work and faithful communicators of His divine message. But is there any evidence that this is the case? Can we objectively examine whether or not the Bible came from God? I believe we can.

Objective evidence

Add up all the major religions of the world and together they will identify about 26 books that they allege to be divinely inspired (or given to us by God). But the Bible stands out from these other books in some very significant ways.

The Bible alone records hundreds of fulfilled prophecies. Only God truly has the ability to tell us the end from the beginning. These prophecies are not lucky guesses or coincidences. Rather, we are given specific details concerning everything from the rise and fall of the great kingdoms of the world to personal information about individuals who would be instrumental in God's plan. There are scores of prophecies given hundreds of years before Jesus Christ's birth that found their amazing fulfillment in Him. As we will see in chapter 4, the Old Testament prophets foretold nearly every significant aspect of His life.

Archeology also lends credence to the Bible, which references hundreds of cities, people and events in both the Old and New Testaments. In the past, many of these factual claims could not be validated by other historical documents and as a result, skeptics had a heyday criticizing the accuracy of the Bible.

However, in the latter half of the twentieth century, it seemed that every turn of the archeologist's spade produced supporting evidence for the Bible. Cities once thought to be hypothetical were unearthed. Kings, prophets and military leaders purported to be mythological showed up in ancient records discovered among the Dead Sea Scrolls and the tablets of Ebla. In fact, there are now literally thousands of archeological discoveries confirming historical aspects of the Bible, and the number of these confirmations continues to grow dramatically.

Making it personal

But there is an even greater way to confirm whether or not the Bible is the actual word of God. You can read it for yourself and discover if it speaks to your heart and soul like no other book ever has.

Many people try to read the Bible by starting with Genesis and soon get bogged down with lengthy genealogies, names they can't pronounce and the exhaustive descriptive instructions of Old Testament law. But you can read and understand the Bible for yourself if you follow a few basic principles:

First, start reading in the New Testament with the Gospel of Matthew. The laws, sacrifices and rituals of the Old Testament have their appropriate place in Bible study, but the life and teaching of Jesus Christ are far more relevant to each of us today. (Note: Matthew begins with a genealogy. There actually is a lot of interesting history in it, but as you begin to read, feel free to skip these first few paragraphs and get right into the birth of Jesus Christ.)

Second, read in a translation you can understand. If you really enjoy Shakespeare, I recommend the King James Version. If not, try a more contemporary translation of the Bible. They all say the same thing – some just say it more in the language of our day.

Third, ask God to help you understand what you're reading. The Bible is the only book in the world where the Author can actually be at your side to help explain it along the way. In simple prayer, ask God to reveal the truth to you, to help you know what is being said. Tell Him that you are willing to believe and follow whatever He clearly shows you.

Fourth, set a simple schedule for reading. Don't let your good intentions fall by the wayside. Set apart 10 to 15 minutes a day – perhaps in the morning, at lunchtime or before going to bed – and stick to it for the next 30 days. You'll be surprised how much you learn in this brief time.

The Bible has dramatically changed the lives of millions of people. It can change yours as well! Don't you owe it to yourself to personally read it and discover exactly what it says for yourself?

Contradictions in the Bible?

Who hasn't heard the age-old accusation that the Bible is filled with errors and contradictions? In fact, it has been said so many times that most of us assume it to be true without really checking it out. After all, everyone else couldn't be wrong, could they?

I once carried on a lengthy dialogue with a skeptic named Roger at the University of Maryland. After weeks of disagreement, he greeted me one Monday with a smile on his face and was happy to announce that I had actually motivated him to read the New Testament for himself. I was delighted.

And then, with even greater glee, he told me he had found 27 contradictions in the New Testament that he wanted to show me. We painstakingly went through a first, then a second and finally a third. Each "contradiction" – when read in context – had a simple explanation that Roger had no trouble accepting.

In fact, the answers were so obvious that I finally asked him if he had found these "contradictions" on his own or if someone else had shown them to him. He sheepishly admitted that he hadn't even read any of the New Testament; he had just copied down the list from some book written by another skeptic.

Studied carefully in its context, I do not believe the Bible has a single contradiction concerning any matter of significant teaching. However, we must understand three important words dealing with this discussion: contradiction, paradox and mystery.

A *contradiction* is when "both A and non-A in the same context are claimed to be true." For instance, if the Bible taught in one place that Jesus is the Son of God and taught in another that He is not the Son of God, that *would* be a legitimate contradiction. If it taught in one place that Jesus was the Son of God and taught in another place that a false prophet claimed He wasn't the Son of God, that *would not* be a contradiction. It would merely be pointing out that we shouldn't believe the false prophet.

A *paradox* is when two statements appear at first to contradict each other, but further examination demonstrates that the two statements actually complement each other. For instance, in some places the Bible teaches that Jesus is the Son of God and yet in other places it calls Him the Son of Man. Skeptics may jump on this and ask, "Which was He – the Son of God or the Son of Man?"

The answer is that He was both! The Bible teaches that Jesus is both fully divine and fully human. He is true God and true man. This is the miracle we celebrate at Christmas – the time when God became a man – known to Christians as the incarnation. And to be technically correct, when Jesus used the term "Son of Man," He was referring to a title for the Messiah found in the Old Testament (Daniel 7:13). In calling Himself the "Son of Man," He was actually referring to Himself as divine.

Another paradox confusing to many people concerns the genealogies of Jesus Christ. It doesn't take too much examination to realize that the genealogy given for Jesus in the book of Matthew is very different from that given in the book of Luke. How can that be? This appears to be too big to overlook.

But once again, there really is a simple answer: Jesus had two parents. The genealogy given through Matthew is that of one of his parents and the genealogy given in Luke is traced back through his other parent. After all, I would hope His family tree didn't look like a straight line!

But how do we know which genealogy refers to which parent? It becomes obvious by the themes of each book:

Matthew paints a portrait of Jesus as the King of the Jews. His genealogy would, therefore, be traced back through Joseph, His legal earthly father.

Mark writes of Jesus as the servant of the Lord. He doesn't give us any account of the birth of Jesus.

Luke, a physician, shows us Jesus as a human being. He writes much about the birth of Jesus through the eyes of his mother, Mary. Therefore, it makes sense to conclude that this genealogy is traced back through Jesus' mother.

John writes of Jesus as the divine Son of God. His account of Jesus' birth begins in eternity past when "the Word was with God, and the Word was God" and then goes on to tell us that "the Word became flesh and dwelt among us, and we beheld His glory, glory as of the only begotten, from the Father, full of grace and truth" (John 1:1,14).

The final word we must understand in this discussion is *mystery*. A mystery is something that we cannot comprehend in our limited human understanding, but which is nevertheless true.

An example of this is the controversy concerning predestination and free will – or in other words, does God predetermine our future or do each of us choose our own way? Actually, I believe the Bible teaches that both of these positions have validity.

In our limited minds, we may have difficulty comprehending how both of these can be true at the same time (I know that I certainly do). However, the problem is not with the Bible but with our limited ability as humans. In this case, we are finite beings and we live in a temporal world; these truths are infinite and eternal. Thus, our confusion.

Let me offer a word of advice concerning difficulties in the Bible: never let what you *don't* understand in the Bible keep you from believing what you *do* understand.

We wouldn't allow a fourth grader to reject all of mathematics simply because he couldn't understand calculus. "Learn your addition, subtraction, algebra and geometry," we would tell him, "and some day you'll be able to understand calculus, too."

When it comes to the Bible, however, some people refuse to believe anything unless they can believe everything. "If I can't understand predestination," they proclaim, "then I'm not even going to believe that God exists!" If you approach learning this way, you'll probably never become a Christian (and you will probably do pretty poorly in math as well!).

Yes, the Bible has many *mysteries* and an even greater number of *paradoxes*. But when studied rightly and fairly, I don't think you will find all those *contradictions* that allegedly fill the Bible.

Just being gullible?

People sometimes ask me if I'm gullible enough to believe something just because it's written in a book. Actually, I'm not and I hope you aren't either.

On the other hand, most of what I do know I learned from books. I'll bet that nearly all of the history, science, mathematics and other information that you know you learned from books as well. Rather than simply being guided by our fickle feelings, we can have time-tested and proven information passed on from one generation to another via the printed page.

God does communicate with people in many ways. We've all felt His awe expressed through His creation. We've been guided by His moral laws, which are innately embedded in our consciences. But the most objective and accurate way God has revealed Himself to us is through the Bible.

Generation after generation of people – right down to today – have met God and had their lives transformed through what they have learned from the Bible. It has stood the test of time and passed the credibility test as no other book ever written. If we were to study great books honestly and objectively to determine which one God gave us, I can't think of a book with greater influence, life-transforming power and credibility than the Bible. Can you?

Next, we'll take a look at what this incredible book has to say about a really hot topic these days – the question of who decides what's right or wrong!

Tom Short:
The benefits of reading the Bible

QUESTION 3

Don't I determine what's right for me?

What is the latest atrocity to shock you?

Our newspapers and TV news programs have almost become an assault on our sensibilities. Modern communications bombard us daily with heinous crimes from around the world.

Yet, as we witness more and more corruption and vice, we are being bombarded with another message as well. That message? "Do not judge! Live and let live! No one has the right to say that someone else's behavior is wrong, bad or evil."

Although certain things still repulse most of us, this message of tolerance has been so pervasive that we must wonder is there such a thing as right and wrong anymore? Are there some things that are always wrong for all people at all times in all circumstances – or do we each get to decide what is right for us?

As opposed to the modern philosophy of moral *relativism* (where nothing is ever absolutely right or wrong – it just "depends"), the Bible teaches that there are moral *absolutes* – certain things that are always right or wrong, *no matter what*. Although some people defend even the worst of crimes, basic common sense demands that murder, rape, adultery, theft, fraud, and other crimes are always wrong.

The "Golden Rule"

The biblical standard of moral absolutes is known as the "Golden Rule" – in short, to treat others as you would want them to treat you. There's really no solid argument against this, for while a man may justify his own adultery, he certainly would be outraged if someone else committed adultery with his wife. A person might excuse his own theft, but he wouldn't accept that same excuse if someone else stole something from him.

This Golden Rule is based on the highest moral principle of all – self-sacrificial love. But while inspiring poems, songs and stories about love strike a chord within us, we also face the internal struggle of thinking and acting selfishly. This selfishness is the essence of what the Bible calls sin – or breaking the laws of God.

Some people believe so deeply in moral relativism that they defend behavior that is simply indefensible. I often speak on college campuses where the philosophy of moral relativism is widely taught (and, I might add, even more widely practiced!). There is usually at least one student who is absolutely sure that there are no absolutes.

What about Hitler?

Thinking that perhaps an extreme example will demonstrate that there are at least some absolutes, I usually ask what he or she believes about Adolph Hitler. Was he a bad man? Was he evil? Are you willing to make a moral judgment about him?

I'm amazed at how often these moral relativists will refuse to make such a judgment. In fact, their philosophy drives them to say some things that are absolutely crazy (pardon my judgment)!

"Hitler would not fit well into our social construct," someone will say. "Well, I would never do what he did, but I wouldn't judge him either," says another. "I don't know if he was wrong or not; I never knew the man," explains another. "Hitler was not wrong, he was sick," someone else concludes.

Perhaps the most troubling response I have ever received to this question came from a New Age woman at Southern Illinois University. "Actually," she said, "Hitler acted on his innermost beliefs. He was true to himself. And in that sense, I think you could say Hitler was a *better* person than most of us are."

Now, no one could argue that Hitler wasn't "true to himself," but you could make a pretty good argument that being "true to himself" was, in Hitler's case, not a good thing.

Certainly you do not think Hitler's actions were right, do you? And yet, if there is no God and there are no moral absolutes, why was Hitler wrong?

After all, the German government said that what Hitler did was legal. The law supported his terror. The voice of the people spoke in electing him. He got away with what he did (at least for awhile). Deep in his heart, evidently he felt that what he was doing was good and right – that he would someday be praised as a hero. But in spite of all this, was he right? I hope you respond with a resounding "No!"

If so, you acknowledge that there are at least some moral absolutes. And while you and I may not be guilty of Hitler's extreme acts, we too have acted selfishly and broken God's absolute moral laws.

Who defines morality?

As we saw in chapter one, there is plenty of evidence for the existence of God. If there were no God and each of us were the highest form of life, then each of us could certainly determine his or her own morality. However, if God exists, the definition of morality belongs to Him, not us.

The Bible not only teaches that God exists, but also that each of us was created in His image. This doesn't mean that we look like God physically, but rather that we are made in His moral image. When it comes to morality, we were made to be like God!

For instance, God did not tell us not to murder just because He wanted to make up some arbitrary rule. He told us not to murder because He is the giver of life and He would never take the life of an innocent person. Likewise, God is truthful and therefore He requires us to be honest and truthful ourselves.

Since God in His very essence is love, whenever we act selfishly – instead of acting out of love – we are failing to reflect His moral image. As we have already seen, the Bible calls this failure to reflect the moral image of God "sin." Furthermore, it points out how reflecting God's moral image is a beautiful thing, but that we "all have sinned and fallen short of the glory of God" (Romans 3:23).

Throughout the Bible, God is constantly revealing to us what He's like and therefore what we are to be like as well. Perhaps the most well known and time-tested expression of God's morality is given in a list commonly called the Ten Commandments.

The Big Ten

The "Ten Commandments" are more than just a classic movie starring Charlton Heston. They have served as the foundation for Western culture and law. Additionally, many people hope to get to heaven by keeping them. The Ten Commandments have also become a political "hot potato" as schools and other public institutions determine whether to post them or banish them from their property.

But despite all this controversy, I've found that most people can't even name half of the Ten Commandments! Can you? Keep in mind, this is pretty important, because this is a standard by which God expects a person to live and by which He will ultimately judge each of us. Therefore, let's take a look at each of the commandments and what they mean. The Ten Commandments are found in Exodus 20:1-17.

> 1. *"I am the Lord your God ... You shall have no other gods before Me."*

Simply put, God requires that He be our "God." He expects us to love Him in the same way as He loves us. He refuses to let us displace Him in our affections. This is not selfish or egotistical of God; it is simply proper and right that you and I love and revere the One who gave us life and continues to rule the universe.

> 2. *"You shall not make for yourself an idol, or any likeness of what is in heaven above or on the earth beneath or in the water under the earth."*

We are to know and love God for who He really is. God doesn't give us liberty to believe whatever we want to believe about Him. He expects each of us to seek Him earnestly and if we do, He promises to reveal His true identity to us.

There are many ideas floating around these days about what God is like. He is referred to as everything from a "higher power" to a novel idea. Some religions claim that there are many gods. To some people, nature is god; to others sex, money, power or love is their "god." Even among people who believe in the God of the Bible, there are those who find some of God's qualities embarrassing and thus have remade Him in their own image.

This commandment is vitally important because a person will ultimately become what he or she perceives God to be. Deep inside every human being is a desire to "worship." Worship is not confined to something you do in a church, synagogue or mosque. Worship entails admiration and ascribing "worth" to something. As a person understands and worships the true God, he will grow to be like Him. But if he ascribes ultimate value to something less than the true God, he will ultimately be remade into that false image himself.

3. "You shall not take the name of the Lord your God in vain, for the Lord will not leave him unpunished who takes His name in vain."

This commandment is often broken through mere carelessness. Many people blurt out a curse word about God or Jesus without even thinking. Perhaps after failing a test, being late on a bill payment, getting cut off in traffic, or expressing general anger or disgust with a situation, a person will blurt out the name of God.

Often, when I hear people curse God, I say, "What?" as if I had not heard them. Their puzzled look demonstrates that they did not really think before they spoke – they just cursed by mere habit or instinct. This is exactly what it means to "take His name in vain" – to use His name in a thoughtless, careless way without giving it the proper respect.

In fact, to many people, the name of God is nothing more than a way to express anger or disgust. For years I thought it was cool to cuss. I used all sorts of phrases with my friends that I would never say in front of my mother. Rather than honoring God for who He was, I demonstrated utter contempt for His very name. Jesus said that our words indicate what is in our hearts. When you listen to what you say about God, what does that tell you about the content of your heart?

As an interesting side note, have you noticed how only the Christian names for God ever get used as a curse? Everywhere I've traveled, I've heard "God," "Lord," "Jesus" and "Christ" used in vain. But never any other names. For example, I don't ever remember a teacher handing back tests and one of my fellow students blurting out, "Oh, Buddha!" Nor have I ever heard anyone ask "Allah" to damn someone. Could it be that the mortal enemy of our souls, who knows the name of the one true God, delights to see Him cursed but could care less about other names?

The scariest thing about this commandment is that, even though many people unconsciously break it every day, it is the only one of the ten where God adds a threat of punishment in the same sentence: "...for the Lord will not leave him unpunished who takes His name in vain." Worried? You should be. But read on – we'll find out what to do about it in a later chapter.

> 4. *"Remember the Sabbath day, to keep it holy. Six days shall you labor and do all your work, but the seventh day is a Sabbath of the Lord your God; in it you shall do no work."*

This commandment reminds us of the simple fact that God is the source of life itself. We are to take a day each week for spiritual and physical refreshment. A day to remind us that we belong to God and worship Him accordingly. And yet, some people are so rebellious against God that they won't even obey Him when He tells them to relax!

This commandment is a perfect example of how God's commandments are given in love and are for our benefit. Our world has abundant conveniences to make life easier and simpler. From microwaves to cell phones, computers to cars, machines do much of the work that people used to do. In the 1960's, social scientists pondered what people would do with all of their spare time now that computers and machines were doing so much! And yet, we are more harried, hurried and hassled than at any other time in our history.

> ● Tom Short:
> **How do you choose which Old Testament laws to obey?**
>

Millions of people are afflicted with mental and physical illnesses brought on by stress and anxiety. Believe it or not, there was a day not long ago when hardly anyone worked on Sunday. It was a day reserved for church, family and home life. And it was a day when, in spite of fewer amenities, people were healthier and happier. Perhaps we should learn something from those folks.

5. *"Honor your father and your mother."*

Do you think God was aware of adolescence when He gave us this commandment? I'm sure He was, and I'm also sure He was aware of how difficult it can be to show our parents honor and respect no matter what stage of life we (or they) are in. And yet, God says we are to honor, respect and obey our parents. This does not mean only in a general sense or when we already agree with them, but at all times! Failing to do so is a sin – a very grave sin.

Sometimes people wonder if they are required to honor an abusive parent. Yes, we are to continue to honor them simply because they are the ones who brought us into this world. However, there may be times when, even though we continue to *honor* our parents, we are not to *obey* them. The clearest example would be if our parents required us to do something sinful. Obviously, we are not to obey our parents if it means disobeying God.

6. *"You shall not murder."*

I know what you're thinking: "Finally, we get to a commandment that I haven't broken!" Yes, we've all cursed, violated the Lord's day, followed false concepts of God and dishonored our parents, but at least we haven't *killed* anybody. In fact, I often ask people why they think God should allow them into heaven and a common answer is,

"Because I've never killed anyone."

However, Jesus pointed out that God's standard goes beyond our actions to the attitude of our hearts. Here's what He said: "You have heard that the ancients were told, 'You shall not commit murder,' ... but I say to you that everyone who is angry with his brother shall be guilty before the court; and whoever shall say to his brother, 'Raca' (i.e., "empty-head" or "good for nothing") shall be guilty before the supreme court; and whoever says 'You fool' will be guilty enough to go into the fiery hell" (Matthew 5:21-22).

God is interested in our hearts and our motives. While it might be commendable that you haven't actually killed someone who irritates you, it's your heart that counts. Which of us can say that we have never hated someone, sought revenge, destroyed someone's reputation with our words, or been jealous or envious? These thoughts, words and actions spring from selfishness and fall short of the love God expects us to exhibit.

7. "You shall not commit adultery."

God created marriage and the family. This commandment is designed to protect this vital institution and assure a loving and stable environment for both adults and children.

The Bible considers adultery to be a direct attack upon the family. Likewise, this commandment prohibits all sex before or outside of marriage. Sometimes it seems that people lie awake at night dreaming of ways to violate this commandment while still remaining "technical virgins" or "technically faithful."

Viewing pornography, frequenting strip clubs and fantasizing over romance novels may not involve physical adultery, but they feed the selfish and adulterous heart within us. God is not interested in us keeping the *letter* of the law while violating the *spirit* of the law. (I'll bet your spouse wouldn't be too pleased either!)

Don't get me wrong. Sex is not a bad thing – in fact, it is a wonderful thing. It is the misuse of sex that God condemns. Actually, the very first commandment God gave to Adam and Eve had to do with sex. When He told them to "Be fruitful and multiply," he wasn't referring to gardening and mathematics! And when Adam and Eve enthusiastically did their part to obey this commandment, God wasn't startled into saying, "I didn't mean *that*!"

God's commandments are given to us in love. He gives us His commandments about sexual fidelity not to rob us of pleasure, but rather to provide us with a lifetime of guilt-free intimacy with a life-long spouse. Multitudes of people today suffer deep emotional pain. Can you think of anything that has caused more pain and hurt than God's laws of sexuality being violated either by that person or by someone else close to them?

8. *"You shall not steal."*

We are not to take anything that belongs to another person. It doesn't matter whether we are taking something expensive or of little value. It doesn't matter whether we are stealing from the rich who "wouldn't miss it" or from the poor who would have trouble defending themselves. This includes cheating on a test and cheating on our taxes. We are never to take what belongs to another.

9. *"You shall not bear false witness."*

God is truthful and we are to be, too. We are forbidden to lie about someone or to someone. This commandment also forbids gossip and slandering another person. Our word should be good, whether we have sworn on a stack of Bibles and signed our name to it or not.

10. *"You shall not covet anything that belongs to your neighbor."*

While there is nothing wrong with working hard to get something we want, this commandment forbids us from lustfully seeking (coveting) what is not rightfully ours. It gets to the motive of our hearts and requires us to be content. This is tough in our materialistic world where we are daily bombarded with advertisements for things we're told we need to truly be happy.

⯈ Tom Short:
Did the God of the New Testament change from the God of the Old Testament?

You Tube

This commandment goes beyond coveting material possessions. It includes being content with our looks, intelligence, family heritage, physical stature, etc. Have you ever been jealous of someone else's appearance or brains? Then you've violated this commandment.

Big Trouble

If this is the standard by which God will judge humanity, one look at this list tells me that I'm in trouble – big trouble! I score a perfect 10 with this list – I've broken all of them!

If this were the end of the story, we could rightly conclude that we don't have much hope of making it to heaven. Desperate to be approved by God, some people resort to religion, philosophy or denial of earthly pleasure. Others gamble that if they can just do enough good things to balance out the bad they have done, they'll be safe. I used to think that God couldn't send everyone to hell, so as long as I was in the top 10 or 20 percent of humanity, I would have a pretty good chance of getting to heaven.

Of course, all of these approaches miss one vital point: our moral problem before God has to do with more than just the acts we've committed. It gets down to our very nature of being selfish. And the solution to that problem is far greater than you or I could come up with on our own - which is why it's now time to move on to the fourth question. It just might be the most important one of all.

QUESTION 4

Wasn't Jesus just a great teacher?

I often wonder what people really mean when they say this.

Do they mean that Jesus had a strong, persuasive voice that moved people to action? Do they mean that He had great body language and natural charisma? Do they mean that He used intriguing stories to help ordinary people gain insight into extraordinary spiritual truths?

Since we don't have videotape of Jesus speaking, we'll never know. For all we know, He may have had a high, squeaky voice and been as stiff as a board.

The reality is, Jesus was not a great teacher because of His teaching style – He was a great teacher because of His *message*! And what did this great teacher teach about more than anything else? He taught about Himself!

Many people think that Jesus simply taught to be kind and loving – to care for those less fortunate and to turn the other cheek to your enemy. And He did teach those things in very profound ways. But the heart and soul of His teaching was not a creed or a way of thinking or a set of rules. The heart and soul of His teaching was who He was and what He came to do.

Many famous religious teachers have taught what they understood to be spiritual truth. But they themselves were not the central message.

For instance, you can take Mohammed out of Islam and still have Islam (submission to God). You can take Buddha out of Buddhism and still have Buddhism (enlightenment). You can take Confucius out of Confucianism and still be... confused!

But if you take Jesus Christ out of Christianity, you have nothing left. For He – and He alone – is what Christianity is all about.

> ⏺ Tom Short:
> **What makes Jesus different from other religious leaders?**
> YouTube

Therefore, if you claim that Jesus was a great teacher, you must seriously and carefully consider what He taught about Himself and His mission.

Who He claimed to be

Who do *you* think Jesus was? Was He merely a very good man or was He more than a man? Consider carefully some of the claims that Jesus made about His own identity.

"I am the bread of life; he who comes to Me shall not hunger, and he who believes in Me shall never thirst" (John 6:35). Do you want to taste of real life? You'll find it in Jesus.

"I am the light of the world; he who follows Me shall not walk in darkness, but have the light of life" (John 8:12). Do you ever feel as if life is like trying to walk through a dark room – not seeing or knowing what's in your path? Jesus says He will "turn the lights on" if you follow Him.

"I am the door; if anyone enters through Me, he shall be saved" (John 10:9). Do you ever wonder how to get into heaven? Jesus says He is the door. Not His teaching, not His example, not His organization – but *Jesus Himself*. To enter heaven, you must enter through Jesus.

"I am the good shepherd; the good shepherd lays down His life for the sheep... I know My own and My own know Me" (John 10:11,14). Do you ever want someone wiser and stronger to guide you through life? Jesus is the Shepherd of your soul. But He doesn't just herd you along. He actually demonstrated His love for you by sacrificing His life for you.

"I am the resurrection and the life; he who believes in Me shall live even if he dies, and everyone who lives and believes in Me shall never die" (John 11:25-26). Do you ever wonder what will happen to you after you die? Jesus taught that everyone will experience an eternal existence after he or she dies – in either heaven or hell. Those who have genuine faith in Him are promised that they will rise again to eternal life in heaven.

"I am the vine, you are the branches; he who abides in Me, and I in him, he bears much fruit; for apart from Me you can do nothing" (John 15:5). Have you ever seen a branch that's been broken off from a tree? At first it looks alive and well. But as time goes on, it becomes brittle, hard and dead – obviously separated from its source of life. Do you ever feel like you're separated from the source of real life and your soul is slowly drying up? Jesus claimed that we must be intimately connected with Him if we are to receive true life and nourishment for our souls.

"I am the way, the truth, and the life; no one comes to the Father but through me" (John 14:6). Different people believe there are different ways to God; some think they'll get to God by following a religion, others by adhering to a particular philosophy, others by doing good things for people. But Jesus said none of these things. Jesus claimed that He Himself – a person – was the one and only way to God.

These are not just nice little do-good platitudes – they are truly outrageous claims! Who else throughout world history has dared say such things about Himself? Other religious leaders may have claimed to be prophets or teachers sent to show us the way to live, but only Jesus claimed to be the one and only Son of God who can forgive our sins and give us real life, both now and for all eternity!

Logical conclusions

Based on the astonishing things Jesus taught about Himself, believing that He was simply a good teacher is not an option. He was either seriously deluded or a diabolical liar or the most egocentric, arrogant person to ever walk this earth – or He was telling the truth and was exactly who He claimed to be.

As famed author and former agnostic C. S. Lewis writes in his book *Mere Christianity*:

> *"I am trying here to prevent anyone saying the really foolish thing that people often say about Him: "I'm ready to accept Jesus as a great moral teacher, but I don't accept His claim to be God." That is the one thing we must not say. A man who said the sort of things Jesus said would not be a great moral teacher. He would either be a lunatic - on a level with the man who says he is a poached egg - or else he would be the Devil of Hell. You must make your choice. Either this man was, and is, the Son of God: or else a madman or something worse."*

Got evidence?

Jesus made extraordinary claims, and it is only fair to say that extraordinary claims require extraordinary evidence. Does evidence exist to support the claims of Jesus? Absolutely!

The evidence of fulfilled prophecy

For instance, the Jewish prophets had predicted a coming Messiah for hundreds of years – a Messiah who was to be the hope of the world, who would restore justice and peace to the world, who would reconcile all of the peoples of the world to God.

These prophets spoke in great detail about the Messiah. They foretold His ancestry, the circumstances of His birth, His actions and attitudes, even how others would respond to Him. Incredibly, Jesus fulfilled *all* of their prophecies!

 Tom Short: What does it mean that Jesus fulfilled prophecies?

You Tube

Fulfilling all of these prophecies was nothing short of a miracle! To help us picture just how phenomenal this was, Dr. Peter Stoner, in his book *Science Speaks*, calculated the mathematical odds of Jesus fulfilling just eight of the many prophecies by chance. Stoner didn't choose vague or highly controversial prophecies to up the odds. Instead he chose specific prophecies that are clearly understood, that are not highly controversial and that most people would agree that Jesus fulfilled.

Here are the eight prophecies:

1. He would be born in Bethlehem (Micah 5:2)
2. He would be preceded by a messenger (Isaiah 40:3)
3. He would enter Jerusalem on a donkey (Zechariah 9:9)
4. He would be sold for 30 pieces of silver (Zechariah 11:12)
5. His betrayal money would be thrown into the house of the Lord and then used to buy a potter's field (Zechariah 11:13)
6. He would be silent before His accusers (Isaiah 53:7)
7. His hands and feet would be pierced (Psalm 22:16)
8. He would be crucified with thieves (Isaiah 53:12)

First Dr. Stoner calculated the odds of each individual prophecy being fulfilled by chance, then he multiplied them to find the odds of any one person fulfilling all eight by chance. The odds? One in 1,000,000,000,000,000,000!

How do you get a handle on just how huge a number that is? Stoner illustrates it by calculating how large a space would be covered by 1,000,000,000,000,000,000 silver dollars.

And how large do you think that space is? Well, it's larger than the room you are sitting in – and larger than any house or building you might be in. It's larger than any city or county you are in – in fact, it's even larger than the state you're in. The number of silver dollars is so large that it would actually cover *the entire state of Texas – two feet deep!*

Think of it! The odds of any one man fulfilling just eight of the many prophecies Jesus fulfilled by chance are the same as the odds of you wading into that two-foot layer of silver dollars covering the entire state of Texas and picking the one right silver dollar at random on the first try! Now Texas is a big state (just ask any Texan) and the chance of picking the one right silver dollar is – well, practically impossible. I certainly wouldn't bet my eternal soul on it!

The evidence of miracles

In addition to the prophecies about the promised Messiah, Jesus gave extraordinary evidence of who He was by the miracles He performed. No other religious leader has ever done the things Jesus did. Right out in the open for all to see, He:

- Enabled the lame to walk, the blind to see, the deaf to hear and the mute to speak
- Raised people from the dead – even one man who had been buried for four days
- Turned water into wine
- Fed thousands of people with just a few fish and a couple of loaves of bread
- Calmed a mighty storm with a single word.

These miracles were not mere legends or myths. Eyewitnesses recorded the accounts – and gave details of names, times and places. They were historically accurate and were given as evidence to support the claims of Jesus Christ.

More evidence: the way He died

Another evidence to support the claims of Jesus Christ is the manner in which He died. Jesus believed what He said to the death. Most other great religious leaders simply died of old age, disease, or other natural means. Jesus was killed at age 33 as a direct result of what He taught.

In fact, Jesus was one of the few people in history who was tried and executed because of who He claimed to be. He had claimed to be the Messiah, the Son of the Living God, and the religious leaders of His day simply refused to accept it. Ultimately, they condemned Jesus for blasphemy, because He – in their opinion, a mere man – made Himself out to be God.

Jesus easily could have avoided His cruel execution. He could have said that He wasn't actually claiming to be the Son of God and explained to the religious leaders of His day what He really meant. But He didn't. He knew exactly who He was. And the religious leaders knew exactly who He was claiming to be. Jesus made no attempts to deny the identity He claimed, even when He knew it would cost Him His life.

The final evidence: His resurrection

The final extraordinary evidence provided by Jesus concerns His bodily resurrection from the dead. There are three facts:

1. Jesus lived
2. He died
3. He was buried

And then, there is a fourth fact that has changed the course of history. Three days after He was buried, *His tomb was empty!* His body was gone!

Over the next forty days, hundreds of people testified that they saw Jesus alive again. They talked with Him, ate with Him and touched Him. He appeared at least ten different times, to individuals and groups both large (over 500) and small. He appeared to people who were gathered inside a home and to people who were outside in the open. He appeared to people who were initially very skeptical of the resurrection reports, but who afterwards went out and told the world what had happened.

Thomas, one of Jesus' twelve disciples, was one of those skeptics. His whole world had been shattered when Jesus was crucified. His hopes and dreams broken, he decided to go back to his old life and try to reclaim what he had lost when he decided to follow Jesus.

When he heard reports of the resurrection, he hardened his heart and stated firmly, "Unless I shall see in His hands the imprint of the nails, and put my finger into the place of the nails, and put my hand into His side, I will not believe" (John 20:25).

Eight days later, he got his wish. The disciples were gathered together, the doors were shut and Jesus stood in their midst. He looked Thomas in the eye and said, "Reach here your finger and see My hands; and reach here your hand, and put it into My side; and be not unbelieving, but believing." Thomas responded, "My Lord and my God!" (John 20:26-28). You can bet that "doubting Thomas" didn't doubt again after that!

Are you catching the significance of this? The Bible says that Jesus actually, physically rose from the dead! It is not talking about a "spiritual resurrection" or the idea that even though they killed him he "lives on with us today." Rather, the literal body that was crucified and buried is now alive and well!

But how do we know whether or not it really happened? We know the same way that we know every other event of history – through credible eyewitnesses who are willing to face cross-examination. Just as a jury is convinced by the testimony of eyewitnesses that holds up under the grilling of cross-examination, so the New Testament provides us with numerous compelling, eyewitness accounts of Jesus risen from the dead.

But His followers' "cross-examination" was not as simple as facing a masterful lawyer in the confines of the courtroom. Their cross-examination was very simple: either stop talking about the resurrection or your property will be confiscated and you will be beaten, imprisoned, and ultimately tortured to death.

This is exactly what happened. Of the twelve disciples who were the primary witnesses of the resurrection, eleven suffered cruel and torturous deaths rather than change their story. The twelfth (John) – who had actually survived being dipped in a vat of boiling oil – was abandoned to a deserted island until his natural death.

Don't let the impact of this escape you. These witnesses – people known for their sincerity and integrity – faced the ultimate cross-examination and not one of them ever changed his story.

Plenty of people throughout history have died for a lie, but how many people do you know of who willingly died for something that they *knew* to be a lie? Yet, when facing torture and death, none of the disciples ever backpedaled by saying something like, "Well, we might have simply been seeing a vision," or "I'm not really sure it was Jesus," or "Actually, we made the whole story up." Each and every one of them remained faithful to his eyewitness testimony as long as he could draw a breath.

If you are honest, you will have to admit that there is enough evidence to convince a court that Jesus really did rise from the dead. I realize it's hard to believe. I realize that dead people don't usually rise from the dead. I realize that you've never *seen* someone rise from the dead before. Yet the *evidence* tells us convincingly that Jesus did rise from the dead. Personally, I believe it!

And I'm not the only one who believes. The world has never been the same since Jesus came to earth, lived, died and rose from the dead. More people have believed in Him and followed Him than any leader who has ever lived. Entire nations and cultures have developed around His teaching. Individual lives, communities and even nations have been radically changed because of Him. He has emerged as the single most influential figure of all time. In fact, it wouldn't be out of line to say that history is really "His story."

> ⏵ Tom Short:
> **What about those who have never heard of Jesus?**
> You Tube

The following prose attempts to capture the life and impact of Jesus Christ:

> *Here is a young man who was born in an obscure village, the child of a peasant woman. He worked in a carpenter shop until age 30, and then for three years He was an itinerant preacher. He never wrote a book. He never held an office. He never owned a home. He never had a family. He never went to college. He never traveled more than 200 miles from the place where He was born. He never did one of the things that usually accompany greatness. He had no credentials – but Himself. While He was a young man, the tide*

of public opinion turned against Him. His friends ran away. He was turned over to His enemies. He went through the mockery of a trial. He was nailed to a cross between two thieves. While He was dying, His executioners gambled for the only piece of property He had on earth – His cloak. When He was dead, He was laid in a borrowed grave through the pity of a friend. Nineteen centuries have come and gone, and today He is the central figure of the human race and the leader of the column of progress. I am well within the mark when I say that all the armies that ever marched, and all the navies that ever sailed, and all the parliaments that ever sat, and all the kings that ever reigned, put together, have not affected the life of man upon the earth as has that one solitary life.

— Anonymous

Just a good teacher?

Although there has never been a teacher quite like Jesus, He was far more than just a teacher. Jesus was, and is, the Lord and the Savior who is the solution to our ultimate problem. He Himself is the answer to the spiritual, emotional and relational needs we have, for He has come in order to bring us back into a relationship with God.

A relationship with God – is it possible? What would it be like? We'll explore this question in our next chapter.

QUESTION 5

Isn't being a Christian boring and limiting?

Now we get down to the real issue in many people's minds. Frequently I go through the first four questions with people, only to have someone say something like this:

"Okay, I'll grant you that there is a God. And the Bible does seem to be a pretty amazing book. I'll admit I've done some bad things in life and I see how Jesus died for those sins. Maybe some day I'll get religion... but not now. Hey, I'm young and I've got a lot of living to do! Becoming a Christian would just be too boring and limiting right now."

This certainly is the stereotype of Christians. I've run into people who think that becoming a Christian means you have to stop doing the ten things you enjoy most and start doing the ten things you enjoy least – and doing them all the time!

As one guy at Ohio State told me, "I tried the Christian thing when I went to youth group. Let's face it, you guys are boooorrrrrrrring." In contrast, he told me that for fun he "hangs out" and "does stuff." (Sounds pretty riveting, huh?)

Who wants to be bored?

Nobody wants to be bored. We spend billions of dollars each year trying to avoid this dreaded malady. We see the latest movie with the coolest special effects so that we can laugh or get scared or get shocked or do all three at once. We download the latest music or movie. We go to concerts and games. And if none of that is available, we tune into one of hundreds of cable channels available on our big screen TV with surround sound. Today, the big bucks go to the guys who can make us laugh, cry or "ooh and ah!"

Don't misunderstand me. I'm not saying these things are bad or wrong. But the truth is, these forms of entertainment have become wildly successful for one simple reason – we really *are* bored!

Many of us are bored at work. Our jobs lost their excitement and significance years ago. We stick it out through the daily grind because we've got to bring home a paycheck.

Others of us are bored with our relationships. Somehow they've become cold and stale. The people who should be our most intimate friends simply become strangers we share a house with.

Unfortunately, most people try to deal with boredom the wrong way. I often ask people, "What's the opposite of boredom?" The most common answer is "having fun." People attempt to replace the pain of boredom by filling their lives with fun. Bored people often abuse drugs, alcohol and sex trying to fill the emptiness in their lives. Something that started out as "fun" often ends up making a person feel even more lonely and empty than before.

Beating boredom

There's a better cure for boredom. I believe that the opposite of boredom isn't fun, it's *fulfillment* – knowing your life has purpose and meaning.

Does *your* life have purpose and meaning? Do *you* know why you are on earth? Do *you* have a purpose that is worthy of a human created in the image of God – or are your highest goals no more significant than those of mere animals: survival, pleasure and reproduction?

The Bible contends that God has a purpose for each of our lives. "For I know the plans I have for you," declares the Lord, "plans to prosper you and not to harm you, plans to give you hope and a future" (Jeremiah 29:11).

If you want to overcome boredom, I can't think of any better way than to discover God's plan for your life. Once you know why the Almighty has put you here on earth, your eternal destiny begins to become clear. And when that happens, each day holds something to look forward to. Your goal might not be having fun, but you will have grown to find the meaning in each new day. You will become a *fulfilled* person.

The limits of fun

Millions of people have come to experience this fulfillment through a relationship with God. People used to say that I was the life of the party and, let me tell you, I did have a lot of fun! Yet I remember coming home from many parties feeling very empty. I would lie awake in bed, feeling that there had to be something more to life than just having fun.

I even got involved in worthy social action programs and philosophical pursuits, but I never found lasting fulfillment until I found God. I experienced what Blaise Pascal meant when he said, "God has made each of us with a God-shaped vacuum that can't be filled by any created thing, but only by the Creator Himself, in Jesus Christ."

Of course, one reason it can seem like Christians must not be enjoying life is because God forbids so many things that seem to be fun. The Bible freely acknowledges that sin has its "passing pleasures" (Hebrews 11:25). But many of those "passing pleasures" carry a hefty price tag. God's plan for us includes true and lasting joy without the consequences that come from filling our lives with sinful pursuits whose pleasure never lasts.

This leads us to the second half of our question: *"Isn't being a Christian limiting?"* Actually, this statement has a great deal of truth in it. I'll have to agree that, in some ways, the Christian life is limiting. As a Christian, there are things that God simply tells us not to do – that He restricts us from doing.

But it must be understood that God prohibits us from doing certain things because of His genuine love for us. Just as a good parent won't allow his children to do things that are dangerous, so God provides His commandments for our protection.

For example, His restrictions against hatred pave the way for us to be filled with genuine love for others. His restrictions against sexual promiscuity enable us to someday have a wonderfully intimate relationship with our husband or wife. His restrictions against "getting wasted" protect us from doing things we will truly regret when we sober up. As we saw earlier, God has a plan for our lives – an eternal destiny for each of us – and the last thing He wants is for us to simply waste our potential.

Guardrails for your good

I believe an illustration is in order here. When I lived in southern California, I would occasionally drive my family up into the mountains. Many of the roads wound up the side of very steep inclines. Looking out to my left, I could see that we had a long way to go to reach the top. Looking down into the canyon on my right, I could see that we had already come a long way. I would always cling to the steering wheel, knowing that if our van ran off this narrow mountain road, we would tumble down the canyon to our death.

There was one thing that made this tenuous situation safe and secure. Guardrails! They were placed there to protect us, to keep us on the road, to save us from certain death if we slipped off the path. They provided an assurance that we would arrive safely at our destination.

God's commandments are like those guardrails. Their "restrictions" are for our protection. In our journey through life, they keep us from going over the edge. If we look at things the right way, we can be deeply grateful that God has given us these guardrails. They are for our good; they are given in love; they will allow us to "reach the top of our mountain" and fulfill our destiny in life.

Unfortunately, many of us know people who have jumped the guardrail of life and are urging us to join them. Now plummeting down the side of a mountain may not seem all that bad at the time. In fact, it might seem a lot more exciting than the most extreme amusement park ride! But someday, they will hit the bottom and the ride will be over. They will bear the consequences of their choices. They will look up at the top of the mountain and realize that while others have reached their true potential, they have not.

Funny how it works

I'll acknowledge up front that if your *ultimate* goal in life is to have fun, you probably won't want to become a Christian. But, I'll also warn you that if your ultimate goal in life is to have fun, in the long run you will not be very happy. It is simply one of those mysterious laws of life that true happiness is found less in selfishly seeking things for ourselves and more in unselfishly giving to others.

It takes maturity to understand this, but if you study people who have experienced real happiness in life over the long haul, you'll see that they have been more interested in selflessly giving to others than in selfishly seeking for themselves. Self-centered people end up anything but happy – they end up empty and usually leave a string of shattered relationships along the way.

This brings me back to how I started this book. We all know Christians who seem to be happy, fulfilled and genuinely caring people. And now we've seen that these people aren't so wrong after all. Christians do have a solid intellectual and reasonable basis for their faith in Jesus Christ.

In fact, as we have seen, the evidence – for the existence of God, for the reliability of the Bible and for Jesus Christ being God in the flesh – really is compelling. But it's not enough to simply know this information. Like a critically ill person who neglects life-saving medicine, what you have learned in this book will not help you unless you use it. To discover how what you've just learned can make all the difference in your life, don't miss the next and final chapter.

CONCLUSION
The most important question of all

Since I've tried to answer your questions about Christianity, I feel I've earned the right to ask you a question: Have you personally placed your faith in Jesus Christ as your Lord and Savior?

I'll admit that's a pretty personal question. But I also believe it's the most important question you'll ever face. Let's analyze exactly what this question means by reviewing what we have seen so far:

The Bible teaches that God exists and that He is both real and personal. No one can find true meaning in life unless he or she finds it in relation to God, our Creator and the One who rules the universe.

Each of us has sinned against God. As we look at God's standards, we discover that we have broken God's law –

both the letter of His law and the spirit of it.

There are consequences for sinning against God. The Bible tells us "your iniquities have made a separation between you and your God" (Isaiah 59:2). While we were intended to enjoy a close, personal relationship with God, instead we find that our sins have broken that relationship.

Furthermore, the Bible warns us that "the wages of sin is death" (Romans 6:23). As a result of our sin, we are not only separated from God now, but we are in danger of one day being separated from Him for all eternity in a place known as hell.

Jesus Christ is much more than simply a teacher; He is, in fact, a Savior. As the Son of God, He voluntarily died on the cross to pay for our sins. Since the wages of sin is death, Christ chose to die for our sins – the righteous dying for the unrighteous – in order that He might bring us to God.

This is the ultimate demonstration of God's love for us: while we were guilty and deserving of judgment, Jesus took our punishment upon Himself. Jesus went to the cross in our place and for our good, bearing our sin and the judgment we deserved.

Jesus further demonstrated His unique position as the Son of God by rising from the dead. Because of His resurrection, there can be no doubt that His death on the cross fully paid the penalty we deserved for our sins. He has conquered the one enemy of us all – death!

Your response

But how can all of this change your life? Now that you've heard about Christ, you are left with three potential personal responses:

You can *reject* Christ, telling Him that you're not interested, that you don't feel you need Him, and that you don't want Him to be your Savior and Lord.

You can *neglect* Christ, putting off making your decision until some time in the future. This can be a positive choice if you need more time to seriously consider the impact of your decision and to make sure that you really know what you're doing.

However, this is a poor choice if you're putting off making a decision in the hopes that someday Christ will just go away. To put it rather bluntly, failing to decide to accept Christ has the same eternal effect as rejecting Him.

You can *receive* Christ, by simple faith, embracing Him as your personal Lord and Savior.

The Bible teaches that we come to God through faith in Jesus Christ. Rather than trust in our own good efforts or religious activities as a way to "earn" a relationship with God, we are to believe and trust that Jesus, through His death and resurrection, is the one who brings us back into a relationship with God. Forgiveness and reconciliation with God is far too great a treasure to be earned; it is to be received as a free gift from a Giver who loves us deeply.

That gift becomes ours as we put our faith in Jesus Christ. But faith is far more than a simple intellectual exercise. To come to Jesus as your Savior implies that you are sorry for the way you have sinned against God, that you want Him to forgive you, and that you hope to live differently in the future. Faith in Jesus as your Lord includes recognizing who He is and accepting His rightful position as the God of your life.

Those who make this faith decision to receive Jesus Christ enter into far more than a mere religion – they enter into a personal relationship with God Himself! In a very special way, they each become God's beloved child.

Have you entered into this relationship? *Have you personally placed your faith in Jesus Christ as your Lord and Savior?*

If not, I encourage you to do so right now. The Bible promises that "whoever will call upon the name of the Lord will be saved" (Romans 10:13). You can call on Him right now by sincerely praying a simple prayer like this:

Dear God, I thank you for loving me and reaching out to me. I admit that I have sinned against you; I've done things I'm ashamed of and never do them again. I believe that Jesus Christ died for the sins I've committed and then rose from the dead. Right now, I receive Him as my Lord and Savior. Please forgive me and help me to follow You from this day forward. Amen.

I hope you prayed this prayer and are now genuinely trusting Jesus Christ to be your Lord and Savior. If so, you can be confident – based on what God has promised in the Bible – that your sins are forgiven and that you have begun an eternal, personal relationship with the One who loved you enough to die for you!

Keep on growing

There are many ways you can begin to grow in fully experiencing your new relationship with God. First of all, I encourage you to begin to read the Bible as if God had written it as a personal love letter to you alone.

Just as in any relationship, you get closer to someone by communicating – so deepen your relationship with God by talking with Him daily in prayer and sharing with Him the things that are on your heart.

One of the most important things you can do to grow in your personal relationship with God is to spend time with other people who are also pursuing a close, personal relationship with Him. So ask God to lead you to a church that is actively involved in telling others about the "good news" of Christ and begin attending regularly. And be sure to tell at least one Christian friend whom you respect about your decision – he or she can be invaluable in helping you grow in your new relationship with God!

Finally, I want to thank you for allowing me to work through these five crucial questions with you. I hope you have been as stimulated in reading this book as I have been in writing it. May God bless you and become very real to you as your faith grows stronger day by day.

APPENDIX
More than religion:
How I discovered God personally

A genuine relationship with God! It seemed so foreign to think of knowing God in a personal way. All I had ever known was a "Christian" religion that offered a stale and impersonal God. Despite my protests and desire to sleep in, my parents had done their best to get me to church each Sunday. I now appreciate that guidance in developing my own values, but by my early teens, I no longer saw any reason to go to a church that didn't seem to benefit me or most of the others who attended.

During those teen years, I mixed typical red-blooded American pursuits (sports, academics, money, and, of course, girls) with a spiritual quest to discover how and why I should live. I read books which would help develop those values, including classics by Herman Hesse, John Steinbeck and Kahil Gibran. This spiritual pursuit protected me from many of the overt sins in which my friends indulged, but left me wide open to be snared by one of the most deadly sins of all.

That sin became evident to me in the summer of 1972. One evening, while perusing my bookshelf, I noticed a copy of the New Testament. I considered myself to be a Christian, but realized I had never read the New Testament for myself. Assuming I had heard all it had to say, I had turned to other books for spiritual guidance. But I was a fiercely competitive person and my older brother had read the entire Bible. I wasn't going to let him beat me in anything, so I determined to read it myself.

Within minutes, I reached three significant conclusions

1. What I was reading was not what I had been hearing in church. It was alive and relevant, not dead and boring like the church sermons had been.
2. The Bible was unlike anything I had read before. It possessed a unique authority. Other books raised questions; the Bible provided answers! Deep in my heart, I knew I was reading more than the words of mere men — this was God's message to me.
3. I decided that night that I would live the way Jesus taught.

But that wasn't all I discovered. Several days later, I read the 23rd chapter of Matthew. It was here that Jesus cried out against the sin of religious hypocrisy. He disclosed that many are like "whitewashed tombs." Outwardly they appear beautiful, but inwardly they are full of dead men's bones. Even so, Jesus said, "Outwardly you appear righteous to men, but inwardly you are full of hypocrisy and lawlessness." This condemnation pierced my heart and conscience; the words of Jesus Christ revealed to me that outward goodness was not enough. My very nature was evil in the sight of God. Others might have seen me as a "good person," but God saw my heart and He knew better. The Almighty Judge had declared me guilty and I stood condemned.

That was the first time in my life I became genuinely convinced I was a sinner. Not that I had thought I was perfect or without human flaws, but I certainly hadn't felt worthy of the "woe" Jesus pronounced on those religious hypocrites. Now I knew that if I were to die, I would go to hell.

For the next several weeks my spiritual search intensified. I would lie awake at night asking God to forgive me for every sin I could think of. I felt alienated from God and knew that life would be empty if I could not experience Him personally.

The answer to those prayers came as I discovered how the barrier could be removed and my sins be forgiven. "For God so loved the world that He gave His only begotten Son, that whoever believes in Him might never perish but have eternal life" (John 3:16). The answer was found in Jesus! Not a new philosophy or outlook, but a person. God had sent Jesus Christ so that I might not perish but have eternal life! When Jesus died on the cross, He bore the punishment for sins I had committed and for which I should rightfully be punished. He suffered in my place. He was my substitute. Now, through turning from my sin and putting my faith in Jesus Christ, the barrier between God and me was completely removed. I now have a genuine relationship with God!

I had always had a "head belief" in Christ (i.e. an intellectual acknowledgment of the facts), but had never really trusted Him from my heart. But when I realized I was spiritually lost in my sin, I relied on Him to be my Savior. For me, this was not a highly emotional issue, but nevertheless, it was very real. I had invited Jesus into my life and He didn't let me down.

Nor has He let me down throughout the many years I have followed Him. He has kept His promises to me and proven Himself to be very real and personal.

It is my hope and prayer that you, too, will come to Jesus Christ in such a way as to experience the love, forgiveness and life He has in store for you.

Hope you enjoyed reading
5 Crucial Questions about Christianity

Interested in ordering more copies for those you know?

Many people are looking for answers to the questions addressed in this book. I'm sure you know people who are asking these same questions and who could benefit from the information presented here.

Interested in having Tom speak at your Christian group?

Tom Short is available to speak in churches, college groups and youth groups. He is also available to do evangelistic outreaches on college campuses.

For more information about this book, visit
5CrucialQuestions.com

For more information about Tom, visit
TomthePreacher.com